NON PROFIT DEVELOPMENT GUIDE

BY

LAROLYN "NIKKI" YOUNG

Non-Profit Development Guide © 2018 by Larolyn "Nikki" Young. All Rights Reserved

This document is geared towards providing exact and reliable information in regards to the topic and issue covered. The publication is sold on the idea that the publisher is not required to render an accounting, officially permitted, or otherwise, qualified services. If advice is necessary, legal or professional, a practiced individual in the profession should be ordered.

From a Declaration of Principles which was accepted and approved equally by a Committee of the American Bar Association and a Committee of Publishers and Associations.

In no way is it legal to reproduce, duplicate, or transmit any part of this document by either electronic means or in printed format. Recording of this publication is strictly prohibited and any storage of this document is not allowed unless with written permission from the publisher. All rights reserved.

The information provided herein is stated to be truthful and consistent, in that any liability, in terms of inattention or otherwise, by any usage or abuse of any policies, processes, or directions contained within is the solitary and utter responsibility of the recipient reader. Under no circumstances will any legal responsibility or blame be held against the publisher for any reparation, damages, or monetary loss due to the information herein, either directly or indirectly.

Respective authors own all copyrights not held by the publisher.

The information herein is offered for informational purposes solely and is universal as so. The presentation of the information is without a contract or any type of guarantee assurance.

The trademarks that are used are without any consent, and the publication of the trademark is without permission or backing by the trademark owner. All trademarks and brands within this book are for clarifying purposes only and are the owned by the owners themselves, not affiliated with this document.

Table Of Content

Introduction

Hi,

Everyone wants to run a foundation or an organization. We all have that tingling feeling to want to give back to the community via our Non-profit organizations, that's amazing! However, it takes more than just instinct and guts to establish a successful Non-profit organization, it takes thoughtful planning and several considerations. Your passion can lead to positive impact, but first, you need to form a 501c3.

But how and where do you start? Wouldn't it be great to find the answers to all your questions in one place and learn from a professional who's been in your shoes? This author, Larolyn N Young, understands. She struggled to find the information she needed to start her own nonprofit, "HUGS, Helping You Grow Successfully," an organization that helps foster children transition into adulthood successfully. While Larolyn searched for answers to build HUGS, she wrote this book, determined to help others, like you, through the process. She knows the difficulty you're facing.

Non-profit Development Guide provides an unprecedented step-by-step guide into establishing and running a successful Non-profit organization. Its contents are rich and thoroughly thought-through to help anyone decide when, where and how to run a thriving Non-profit organization in any locality they chose to.

From the bylaws, advantages and disadvantages, research, fundraising process, forming the team, content of business plan, winning corporate sponsorships, Non-profit Development Guide provides you with unmatched details that you'd hardly find in any other book. Pick up this easy-to-read, step-by-step guide today, so you can start making the world a better place. People need you and are waiting for your help!

It is my pleasure to officially welcome you to success as you have just taken a step closer to achieving your mission and vision for your organization by downloading this book. Once you are ready, this author extends an invitation to use the consulting services of Key Change., LLC. Larolyn is also the founder/owner of a consultancy that targets it's services to Non-profits. I wish you the very best as you take considerable actions after reading this book. Read, Reflect and Take Actions! Cheers!!!

Respectfully
Larolyn "Nikki" Young, MBA MSHS

HUGS, Helping You Grow Successfully Inc, was created to help college-bound, at-risk and foster youth transition into adulthood successfully. HUGS implements a holistic approach for youth and provides a safe place to access community resources. www.hugscharity.com

Key Change, LLC was created to further assist the business development being your one stop shop for document development and strategic planning for budding Non-profits. They are positioned to assist with every aspect discussed in this guide and more. www.keychangellc.com

CHAPTER ONE:
What Is Non-Profit Organization?

A non-profit organization (NPO) is one which is not driven by profit but by dedication to a given cause that is the target of all income beyond what it takes to run the organization. Non-profit organizations are often used for trusts, cooperatives, and advocacy, and charity, environmental and religious groups.

Many but not all NPOs have paid staff in management positions; almost all use volunteers. NPOs have no owners for surplus profits to go to and any surplus after operating expenses are used to further its goals instead of being distributed between members or employees of the organization. For an NPO to qualify as a government-recognized and tax-exempt organization it has to fulfill conditions set out by government agencies. In the United States, the IRS determines the validity and tax status of NPOs.

NPOs often rely on the dedication of employees who believe in their cause because its hard for them to compete with private sector wages. On the other hand, executive salaries are often quite high as a means of competing with equivalent positions in the private sector.

Funding can be an issue for non-profits as they often rely on external sources, such as donations. Scrupulous accounting, transparency, and accountability are essential to the continuation of operations, as mismanaged or misdirected funds could result in the loss of funding from both public and private sources and loss of status.

Non-profit and not-for-profit are both widely used to refer to NPOs but there are subtle differences. The United States Internal Revenue Service (IRS), for example, uses not-for-profit to refer to activities like hobbies in which revenues are not involved.

The terms NPO and NGO (non-government organization) are also often used interchangeably but they are different. NGOs are separate from government and require no government council but depend on the government for funding. However, most NGOs are also non-profit organizations

Non-profit corporations are often termed "non-stock corporations." They can take the form of a corporation, an individual enterprise (for example, individual charitable contributions), unincorporated association, partnership, foundation (distinguished by its endowment by a founder, it takes the form of a trusteeship), or condominium (joint ownership of common areas by owners of adjacent individual units incorporated under state condominium acts).

Non-profit organizations must be designated as nonprofit when created and may only pursue purposes permitted by statutes for non-profit organizations. Non-profit organizations include churches, public schools, public charities, public clinics and hospitals, political organizations, legal aid societies, volunteer services organizations, labor unions, professional associations, research institutes, museums, and some governmental agencies.

Non-profit entities are organized under state law. For non-profit corporations, some states have adopted the Revised Model Non-Profit Corporation Act (1986). For non-profit associations, a few states have adopted the Uniform Unincorporated Non-Profit Association Act. Some states exempt non-profit organizations from state tax and state employment programs such as unemployment compensation contribution. Some states give non-profit organizations immunity from tort liability (see Massachusetts law giving immunity to a narrow group of non-profit organizations) and other states limit tort liability by enacting a damage cap.

State law also governs solicitation privileges and accreditations requirements such as licenses and permits. Each state defines non-profit differently. Some states make distinctions between organizations not operated for profit without charitable goals (like sports or professional association) and charitable associations in order to determine what legal privileges the respective organizations will be given.

For federal tax purposes, an organization is exempt from taxation if it is organized and operated exclusively for religious, charitable, scientific, public safety, literary, educational, prevention of cruelty to children or animals, and/or to develop national or international sports. Social security tax is also currently optional although 80 percent of the organizations elect to participate.

Advantage And Disadvantage Of Non- Profit Organization

Employee Commitment

Many employees who work for nonprofits have a personal interest in and commitment to the organization's cause. For example, a woman whose relative or close friend fought breast cancer may look for a career opportunity with the nonprofit foundation. A parent whose child is active in scouting may enjoy a staff position with the Boy Scouts of America. There is an advantage to employing workers who believe in the nonprofit's mission, values, and philosophy. In addition, employees with a personal interest may have a better understanding of the structure and processes of a nonprofit organization.

Intrinsic Rewards

The services that nonprofit organizations provide benefit communities and segments of the population that are often overlooked or underserved, such as homeless children. Research conducted by The National Center on Family Homelessness indicates that more than 1.5 million children in the U.S. were homeless in 2005, and the number is expected to rise dramatically due to the effects of a recession.

It's impossible to measure the tangible effects a nonprofit organization can have on families, but the intangible benefits far outweigh the dollar value of their services. Nonprofits and their employees reap intrinsic rewards from the satisfaction of helping clients and community members who are not in a position to fend for themselves. This is a distinct advantage for nonprofits and the people associated with nonprofit organizations.

Disadvantage:

Limited Funding

Fund development and fund-raising can be a nonprofit organization's greatest challenge, particularly during an economic downturn and when unemployment rates are high. In fact, some nonprofits are forced to discontinue services to populations in need when the nonprofit itself lacks funding. Fund development also requires a competent grant writer with a relatively high success rate. Hiring the services of a grant writer can be costly and turn the fund development hurdle into an essential gamble.

Social Pressure

Potential backlash and social fracas plague some nonprofit organizations whose missions are considered extreme, whether they are based on fundamentalist beliefs or progressive attitudes. For example, religious-focused nonprofits whose actions incite an emotional response to the privacy of fallen soldiers and their families receive social pressure to cease activities. Progressive organizations who goal is to enlighten communities and expand the concept of diversity through redefining family structure also encounter protests and opposition to their causes and philosophy.

Other Overlooked Advantages And Disadvantages Of Non-Profit Organization

1. Eternal Life: Nonprofit organizations (just as for-profit organizations) can exist long after their founders leave as long, as their purpose stays relevant and they continue to generate revenue. The oldest company in the world, the Kongō Gumi Construction Company in Japan has been around for nearly 1,500 years.
2. Organization at Scale: If you are a mission-driven individual who wants to make the world a better place, organizing a nonprofit around your chosen cause is the best way to build a team to expand your efforts and make a bigger impact.
3. Protection from Personal Liability: Employees of nonprofits are not personally liable for the debts of the nonprofit. This means that if someone wants to sue your nonprofit for a business-related debt, or injury, they can only go after the corporate entity, not the personal assets of its owners.
4. Tax-Exempt Status of Net Income: Nonprofits do not pay taxes, so all earnings can be cycled back into the organization to improve it.
5. Public and Private Incentive to Help You Out: Donations made by individuals and corporations

are tax-deductible, thereby incentivizing people to contribute to nonprofits. All you have to do is create a clear mission and a strategy to collect donations. I will cover both of these areas in this article.

6. Grants Eligibility: An additional source of funding for nonprofits is through   government grants.

7. Employee Benefits: If your nonprofit has enough employees, it may qualify for group discounts to health or life insurance benefit programs.

8. Formalized Structure: Incorporating a nonprofit can allow you to create formalized roles with job descriptions and responsibilities, which can attract more professional and skillful candidates to work with you.

9. Volunteer Board Members: Typically, nonprofits do not pay their board members, which can save a lot of money. Another pro about board members is that they bring a variety of valuable skills, expertise, and greatly expand your network.

10.   Highly Motivated Employees: Research shows that nonprofit employees are highly motivated by intrinsic rewards like achievements of their clients and a good work/life balance, rather than pay. This means you can expect to attract employees who

care about your nonprofit's purpose and want to help you make a difference in the world.

Disadvantages of Non-profit Organization

1. Time and Money: Starting a nonprofit is likely to take months of preparation and devoted work. It can also cost up to $800 just to submit your application to the IRS. Depending on your bandwidth and knowledge, you may need to hire a consultant to make sure you're filing everything correctly.

2. Continued Maintenance: All nonprofits are required to submit annual filings and comply with all laws of incorporation. There are also quite a few activities which may jeopardize a nonprofit's status (like lobbying). Note that legal requirements differ from country to country. See here for Canadian requirements.

3. Prohibition from Political Campaigning or Lobbying: nonprofits which engage in attempts to influence legislation to risk their tax-exempt status.

4. How to start a nonprofit Public Scrutiny: Anyone may request copies of any nonprofit's filings and review their expenditures, salaries, and income. If your nonprofit will have a large public facing, you

can expect some scrutiny over how you handle administrative expenses. There are always articles about overpaid nonprofit CEOs being published. Just take a look at this image that showed up in my Facebook feed and received hundreds of comments (whether true or not).

5. No Profits: No individuals or shareholders can receive profits from your nonprofit. This can make it more difficult to generate interest from potential investors.

6. Volunteer Board Members: Volunteer Board Members can be a pro and a con. From a con perspective, sometimes it may be had to activate your volunteer board to contribute to achieving goals.

7. Funding Difficulty: While listed as a pro before, getting funding for your nonprofit can be a constant struggle. Given that there are over 1,500,000 nonprofits in the US alone, there is high competition to receive funding from donors, funds, and grants. Many nonprofits hire professional grant writers to give themselves a better chance.

8. Overworked Employees: Small to medium-sized nonprofits typically have tight budgets and only a handful of employees, meaning more work for less pay. It's a scenario some are calling "The Plight of

the Overworked Nonprofit Employee." If these advantages and disadvantages are in line with your expectations of starting a nonprofit, the next section will cover everything a new nonprofit needs to be successful.

CHAPTER TWO:
How to Start Non-Profit Organization

Sometimes, you do whatever it takes to the point of starting a non-profit organization when you believe in a particular cause. Well, this is definitely a noble act but starting a non-profit organization is not easy as you may think it is. It requires great passion, hard work and a lot of help from people around you. In this article, we will discuss various tips on how to start a non-profit organization.

Think positively

The first step that you should take is to set your mind positively. You must have positive thoughts, views, and outlook about the program. You cannot expect to succeed if all you think about is that you cannot do this. To start a non-profit organization, you must take away all the negativities in yourself. You must have the highest hopes that everything will turn out great. As they say, "whatever is going on in your mind is what you are attracting."

Come up with easy business plan template

Just like in running a business, you must have a business plan for the non-profit organization. You should have concrete plans for your goals, mission/vision, marketing strategies, execution of plans and others. When doing your business plan template, you should consider as if you are doing a plan for a for-profit business. Well, you basically have the same principles - you aim to attract investors to fund your programs.

Identify groups or communities that could support your cause

It is also important to determine different groups or communities around your area that may be willing to support your cause. Of course, you need a workforce to materialize all your plans. Therefore, it is advisable to talk to different organizations or groups in your area, share your thoughts with them and see how

Seek for investors and other ways to fund your programs

Of course, it is very important to seek help from the investors to fund your organization. You could pitch to powerful and influential people in your town to be able to get their support. You should use the business plan template that you accomplished.

Contact existing non-profit agencies around your community

Well, this is a very crucial step so you must be very careful. It is recommendable to contact existing non-profit agencies that serve one or more socioeconomic purposes for additional help but you must be very careful not to tap groups with the same or opposite agenda. Talking to existing non-profit groups that work on the same agenda as you may not be ideal because they might feel threatened by your presence thus can affect your status considering that you are just starting. It is the same thing with non-profit organizations with opposing agenda. Therefore, you must do your research first before talking to other non-profit agencies or groups.

You will be able to have an easier time starting your non-profit organization by following the tips mentioned in this article. You should make sure that you have a genuine concern for the cause or program that you are supporting because if not, then you will surely have a difficult time dealing with all the details and things to accomplish for this non-profit organization.

Things To Research Before Starting A Non-Profit

Are you setting up a non- profit organization? Don't forget the specific, technical research you must do to set up a new non-profit organization. Although they will vary on your location, this chapter will give you guidelines for setting up American non-profit Organizations.

Determine If There Are Other Non-Profit Organizations In Your Area That Do Similar Work

Before you start a nonprofit, you should answer the following questions: Is there a need for my organization?

What do I hope to accomplish through my organization? What type of services will my organization provide?

Are there any other organizations doing what I want to do? If so, how will I compete with those organizations?

If another organization is providing a similar service, make sure there is something different about your approach before starting another nonprofit. Your organization will compete with more established organizations for funds to support your work, clients to serve, volunteers to help your organization, etc. Nonprofit organizations are competing for the same limited funds from foundations, major donors, and corporations. In the current economy, the competition has increased and will only get stiffer throughout the year.

Consider Working For an Organization That Does Similar Work

After you do market research, you may find there are other organizations in your area that are doing the type of work that interests you. At that point, you should consider working at the organization to help them fulfill their mission. If you do not want to work at the organization full time, you can volunteer or serve on the board of directors.

Consider Collaborating With an Established Non-Profit

Collaborating with an organization that works in the same issue area is an alternative to starting a new nonprofit. Meet with established organizations to discuss the possibility of partnering on a special project or initiative. Additionally, research national nonprofit organizations in your interest area and determine if a local affiliate is needed in your community. If your community could benefit from a local branch, contact the national headquarters to discuss the idea of bringing the organization to your region.

Move forward with starting a non-profit organization, only after you conduct thorough market research and determine your organization will address a social need that is not being confronted by another non-profit.

501-c-3 or Fiscal Sponsorship?

Perhaps your nonprofit organization is thinking about being officially recognized by the federal government. You have heard terms like non-profit, tax-exempt and 501(c) (3). You wonder what government recognition might mean for your group. What are the benefits? What will it cost in dollars and time?

The IRS Grants Tax Exempt Status

The IRS grants a qualified charity status to nonprofit organizations. The IRS is seeking to discover if a charity is legitimate and they will check for a Board of Directors, bylaws, a mission statement and a budget that does not seek personal gain for the founders. The tool the IRS uses is a 28-page application called Form 1023. The IRS also requires a $300-$750 application fee based on the size of the organization and annual reporting, again based on the size of the organization. It is frequently suggested that organizations get legal and accounting assistance in preparing the Form 1023 application. Becoming a formally recognized not-for-profit organization involves a lot of government paperwork, so an organization must ask if they desire the benefits of 501(c)(3) status and if they are prepared to carry out the responsibilities.

Benefits of 501c3 status

Tax exemption If your organization has a financial surplus (and I recommend that you do have a surplus for emergencies), that profit will be subject to tax unless you file for and receive tax-exempt status from the IRS. Tax exemption is not automatic simply because you are a nonprofit; it must be applied for and granted by the IRS.

Contributions

One of the greatest benefits of 501(c) (3) status is not for the charity, but for its donors. Any contributions of cash or property to a qualified charity are tax-deductible. This is an important benefit that many organizations pursue the paperwork of 501(c) (3) status simply to receive more donations. If your group is not receiving donations (i.e., if you are funded by member fees), you may not need to pursue the 501(c) (3) status. But if you have individuals or businesses that wish to make donations, but will not unless they are tax deductible, you will need the IRS coveted qualified charity status. Also, if you are seeking government or charitable foundation grants, you will need 501(c) (3) status. And, finally, some fundraisers are only open to 501(c) (3) organizations.

Discounts

There is other benefits of 501(c) (3) status including special discounts on postage and some discounts for rent or equipment offered to charities by businesses. Some states offer special status to non-profits such as sales-tax exemptions on purchases made by the nonprofit or property tax exemptions. Check with your state Attorney General's Office to see if they grant special benefits to 501(c) (3) organizations.

Prestige

One intangible benefit of the 501(c) (3) status is the prestige. A 501(c) (3) non-profit organization is serious in their mission, expect to be around awhile and they went to extra effort to be accountable. 501(c) (3) status gives donors assurance that the nonprofit is trying to run a responsible organization.

Here is a quiz to see if you would benefit from 501(c) (3) Status: Do you consistently make a financial surplus (i.e. a profit)?

File for tax-exempt status so the government does not try to tax your profit. Tax exemption is not automatically granted because you are a nonprofit; it must be applied for and granted by the IRS. State governments will also exempt nonprofits from state taxes when they are recognized 501(c) (3) organizations.

Do you have donors who want a tax deduction?

Only organizations that have been approved by the IRS can tell donors that their gifts are tax deductible. The coveted 501(c) (3) status granted by the IRS is essential if you begin accepting donations and someone asks for a receipt. Getting a 501(c) (3) status is a lengthy, time-consuming process, but may be worth your efforts if it increases donations.

Does your group wish to apply for or receive grants?

Granting organizations whether private foundations, corporations or government agencies almost always require 501(c) (3) status.

Does a fundraising program require 501(c) (3) status?

Some programs like local grocery rewards programs require that a group be a 501(c) (3) tax-exempt organization. These reward programs are a great and easy fundraiser, and many nonprofit groups wish to take part. You will need to file for tax-exempt status to participate

To get up and running quickly, many non-profits begin as fiscally sponsored projects operating under the umbrella of a

501-c-3 fiscal sponsor with the stated purpose of serving the public through organizations like yours. The fiscal sponsor will let you collect tax- exempt donations by taking a processing fee, often a percentage of the funding dollars raised. They will also offer a shorter application process and administrative support for your organization as it gets up and running. With this start-up support, you will be in a better position to apply for your own 501-c-3 status at a later date.

Board Of Directors

The appointed board of directors has the authority and responsibility to run the non-profit, usually by selecting and advising the non-profit's executive director. As they can be held legally liable for the activities of the non-profit, it is in their best interest to run the organization safely and legally to avoid risk. Some states require only a minimum of one director, who can be the executive director of the organization, while others require at least three. In any event, building a devoted and responsible board over time can ensure that the fundraising and management capacity of your non-profit continues to develop.

The board of directors of a for-profit corporation is quite similar to a nonprofit organization, but there are a few important distinctions. In general, the fact that both types of businesses are organized as corporations make them fundamentally similar. Members of each have the same fiduciary duties and they must attend to similar governance and operational tasks. Corporate boards are also responsible for complying with state and federal regulations of corporations, such as employment laws and the appropriate IRS filings.

The differences between for-profit and nonprofit boards stem primarily from the obvious differences between for-profit and nonprofit businesses -- their purpose for existing. For- profit corporations exist to make a profit. They can alter or modify the direction of the company at will because anything they do to improve profitability meets the stated purpose, to make money.

Nonprofits, however, must serve a public-service purpose, such as provide education, address the ill-effects of poverty, or serve some other charitable purpose. Nonprofits are accountable to the public, work for the public, and must use all income for the set expenses to meet their stated purpose. To that end, there are some variances in the way a nonprofit board is developed and run that keep the venture in line with its purpose.

Board of Directors Compensation

First, the members of nonprofit boards are not generally paid for their service, whereas for-profit board members typically are. The volunteer capacity of a nonprofit board member does not reduce their responsibility or increase their liability protections. In fact, because the nonprofit board members essentially work for the public, their actions can be scrutinized even more carefully than for-profit board actions. Those who volunteer to serve on nonprofit boards tend to have a personal connection to the efforts of the organization. They are willing to put in the hours to contribute to solving the problem at hand, with no payoff except the satisfaction of charitable work. For-profit board members are also a stockholder, or owners of the business, who are driven by maximizing the profit for their own gain.

Board of Directors is Hands-On

Generally, members of for-profit boards set the standards for the company (profitability goals, etc.) and leave the actual sales efforts to the appointed CEO and his staff. Nonprofit board members are expected to be far more hands-on in developing the funding strategies of the organization. They should solicit funds from their own contacts as well as be involved in major fundraising events. For many nonprofits, the efforts of the board members provide the bulk of capital on which the organization operates.

Non-profit Executive Director

In for-profit corporations, the CEO generally sits on the board of directors. Because all board positions are paid, there is less conflict in regards to the board handling the CEO's salary and job performance. In addition, the CEO and board members all directly benefit from the corporation's profitability.

In a non-profit corporation, the executive director is usually the highest-ranking member of the organization who is actually paid. They are also hired and managed by the board, but since the purpose of a nonprofit does not directly benefit the executive director or board, it makes sense that the executive director is not a member of the board. That is, the unpaid board members are better able to make the best decisions for the organization without the inclusion of the only participant with a personal stake such as the executive director and their salary.

Maintaining Nonprofit Status

The other obvious difference between for-profit and nonprofits are the tax exemption and charitable status available to nonprofits. The board of a nonprofit is responsible for establishing and maintaining each status. One important issue is to monitor the members' self-interest in the activities of the organization. That is, a board member can contract to do work for (and be paid by) the organization, but only within reason and only if the organization can show it did its due diligence before agreeing to the contract. For example, if a board member is hired to design and manage the organization's website, there must be evidence that the board member was selected after careful consideration, and that hiring the board member is the best option for the nonprofit.

Because of the fundamental differences between for-profit and nonprofit corporations' purposes, there are a few distinctive differences in the way these boards are run. Overall, however, the board members retain very similar responsibilities and tasks...after all, business is business no matter where the profits go!

Corporate Bylaws

Most non-profit organizations are required to create official bylaws. This document details the rules that govern your organization at the board level, such as how meetings are run and how decisions are made. There is no need to create this kind of document from scratch, as templates are readily available and generally refer to the famous Robert's Rules of Order as the method for running meetings.

What Are Bylaws?

Bylaws are the technical rules that govern how a corporation will be run. They are a private document for the corporation and are not filed with any government entity. The purpose of the bylaws is to set out how things such as meetings, voting, and share transfer will occur with the business.

Provisions

Typically, the bylaws will be the biggest document in your corporate book. If you are a single shareholder entity, they tend to be fairly straightforward since there isn't really any dispute possibility unless you have a split personality. If there are two or more shareholders, however, the document is going to be a key item because it is going to detail voting rights and so on.

All Corporations should have bylaws. The emphasis is on should because state and federal law doesn't do much to mandate much of anything to do with bylaws.

The bylaws are important as a non-profit because they are going to contain all of the essential information which the IRS requires to know about how your corporation is to be governed and operated. As you will learn, the bylaws are a necessary part of your business in that they provide you and your organization with the procedures you are to follow during operations. In other words, writing your bylaws will make you think through a lot of likely scenarios you wouldn't have otherwise, allowing you to come up with solutions for future problems.

The following information which will be required for your form 1023 (request for tax exemption) should also be a part of your bylaws:

1. Information on the compensation and other financial arrangements with your officers, directors, trustees, employees, and independent contractors.
2. Your conflict of interest and compensation approval policies.
3. Information on your members and other organizations and individuals who receive benefit from you.
4. Your specific activities.
5. Information outlining your internal controls.

Think of the bylaws for your corporation like the Constitution of the United States, and your directors like the members of Congress. Your bylaws will govern the corporate law that dictates how your corporation will be run.

If there is a new treasurer in the company, he is not a director, and he violates the conflict of interest policy, the board of directors will leverage the bylaws to punish him appropriately. The articles of the bylaws state-specific rules by which the corporation operates. In the conflict of interest issue with the new treasurer, there is a specific article that outlines the conflict of interest policy. The policy acts like written law and the boardroom like a court.

The reason that the bylaws should be completed before the Form 1023 is submitted to the IRS is that it contains the internal controls and segregation of duties which the IRS will want to see before they are comfortable with granting you tax exempt status.

If you don't have a conflict of interest policy and policy for approval of compensation, for example, then the IRS would be running the risk of you paying yourself too much money and ripping off your own non-profit company by using it as a front for personal profit. This is an extreme example, of course, but a perfect depiction of why it may be easy to incorporate, but not to get tax-exempt status from the IRS. The IRS certainly does its due diligence to ensure that 501(c)(3) organizations are not defrauding the government to profit personally.

CHAPTER THREE:
Steps To Starting A Successful Non-Profit Organization

If you are passionate about improving your community or desire to make a sustainable difference in the world, then forming a non-profit organization could be the right choice for you. A non-profit is just that not for profit, which means an extra profit and income may not be divided up and distributed amongst members at the end of the fiscal year. While your non-profit organization can most certainly have employees, all leftover revenue is meant to support the cause for which the non-profit was formed. So if the non-profit organization/corporation had a net income at the end of the year of $200,000, it would pay federal and possibly state corporate income tax rates for that $200,000 because it has no shareholders for that profit to be distributed among. This is why many non-profit organization/corporations that have a tax-exempt purpose utilize a 501c3 designation with the IRS, becoming exempt from paying taxes on that $200,000, so they can keep as much of the money they collect as possible and use it to further their organizational purpose.

When you decide to form a non-profit organization, be aware that there are changing factors from state to state for non-profit organization/corporations. Each state is different and it is highly important that you contact the correct offices, obtain the right registrations, and make sure that you are operating in compliance with your state's specific rules.

These steps will get those who are passionate about a cause either in their community or beyond on the right track to making a difference by way of a nonprofit corporation:

Decide On A Name And Address For Your Non-Profit Organization

The name requirements vary, so research your state's guidelines for what's appropriate when it comes to naming your non-profit organization. The differences in name requirements can be down to the word or letter, so pay close attention to detail. All states do require, however, that the name of the non-profit organization is not deceptively similar to or the same as the name of another non-profit or other business entity already registered to do business in that state. Many states give you the option to do an entity name search via their government website. As a new nonprofit without a lot of name recognition, you will find fundraising easier if the name of your nonprofit is relevant to the purpose of your organization.

Consider buying at least the .com .net and .org versions, so no one else can use them. You can shop for URLs at sites like aPlus.net. (Once you have your name and a logo, consider trademarking them to protect your brand.)

Organize Your Team

It is essential to gather a team of like-minded individuals who will work together towards the same goal. Gather a group who is motivated and wants to achieve the same goal, and is passionate about the purpose of the non-profit organization. Figure out who is going to do what within the non-profit: who is going to take care of legal paperwork and compliance reports, who is going to fundraise, who is going to manage employees, who is going to be the leader, who is the good communicator, who is going to be in charge of operations, etc. It is wise once you have assembled your initial team to outline what skills you are missing and search out possible candidates that have these skills and interests. Many business owners will be more than happy to be on a board and help with something they are good at if they share your concerns and vision. Your nonprofit will need incorporators (the person(s) or professional service who files the articles of incorporation with the state to legally form the corporation), directors, and other board members in order to legally operate.

Draft Bylaws

Create laws for your non-profit organization. These are referred to as bylaws. They will not only help govern your nonprofit organization's daily routine and actions, but they will also dictate how officials are elected within your non-profit and will need to elaborate on how assets will be distributed should your nonprofit dissolve. It is wise to seek the legal counsel of an attorney who is well-versed in the law of the state in which you are forming your non- profit, or use a comprehensive non-profit corporation bylaws template to guide you. When it comes time to apply for federal tax exemptions, the bylaws will need to be attached to the application.

An important note about nonprofit corporation bylaws versus for-profit bylaws is a for-profit corporation generally has the power to operate in whichever way they please unless the bylaws eliminate this power. The same goes for the board of directors and officers of a for-profit corporation. Because a nonprofit corporation will typically attempt to obtain tax-exempt status, the IRS will look for specific intentions and language concerning the purpose and goals of the non-profit. The IRS will want to see a short set of very specific reasons the non-profit is formed in order for it to obtain tax- exempt status The primary importance of nonprofit corporation bylaws is to specifically set forth a few powers that the nonprofit corporation and its directors can do and eliminate the rest to comply with the IRS standards for tax exemption

Name A Registered Agent

You must have a registered agent in order to operate a non-profit or any US business for that matter. The registered agent is the individual person or business entity that accepts official state documents on behalf of your nonprofit, such as service of process. Some states allow you to be your own registered agent, and some do not. For non-profits organization that is made up of volunteer board members that have regular jobs, hiring registered agent services from a company is particularly important in order to avoid having board members personally be listed as the agent and having to list their personal residence address.

Nonprofit boards can change frequently, and having to update registered agent addresses with each change of the board can be time-consuming and cause vital state notices to go to old addresses or board members that might not be involved in the nonprofit anymore. Many professional registered agents will also provide compliance tools to help remind the board of due dates. A registered agent service should have an online system to input all the emails and contact info of the board of directors to make the process seamless.

Incorporate Your Non-Profit Organization

You will need to file formation documents in the state in which you are incorporating. In most states, these are called the articles of incorporation. Generally, you will file with the secretary of state or attorney general, though that is subject to differ depending on the state. Most states have official incorporation documents you can download or file online, though Nebraska and Iowa do not. Check out the secretary of state's website in the state in which you are incorporating and you will find more detailed, specific information concerning incorporation in that state. You must make sure to include specific language stating the charitable purpose of your nonprofit on your articles and bylaws, so that you may file for and receive federal tax-exempt status. The IRS has specific laws dictating what language must be used.

Hold An Official Meeting

At this meeting, your team will officially adopt the bylaws for your nonprofit. At this meeting, you will also officially elect the directors and the other officers (such as president, secretary, treasurer, etc.) needed to run your non-profit organization. You will be specifying important things like the real purpose of the nonprofit and making any corporate resolutions needed to complete the process of starting a nonprofit.

ApplyFor Tax Exemption

As a non-profit, you can apply for 501c tax-exempt status at the federal level with the IRS. You will also need to obtain an Employer Identification Number (known as an EIN) from the IRS. The EIN will be used forever to identify your business and you will need one if you hire employees or open a bank account, and for the filing of tax returns. Often, applying for federal tax-exempt status will enable your nonprofit to be eligible for other state tax exemptions as well. Many states do not have processes anything like the IRS. Many states you will just fill out a simple application and include the status letter the IRS gave you showing tax exempt status.

Be AwareOf Strange Requirements

Arizona, Georgia, Nebraska, Nevada, New York, and Pennsylvania all require that new businesses publish in a newspaper before operating in that state. Also, certain states require an initial report to be filed as opposed to just an annual report. There are also certain permits and licenses that must be obtained depending on the state and the city in which you're non-profit is operating.

Start Fundraising for Your Cause

Many states require registration with either the secretary of state, attorney general, or another state office that deals with charities and charity registration. This generally must be done before your nonprofit organization holds its first fundraiser or starts accepting any donations. It is important to have this registration because not only will it help legitimize your nonprofit in the eyes of the donors, but having this certification will allow donors to deduct their donation.

Formulate Your Goalsand Mission Statement

You will need this mission statement later as you file various documents. Your mission statement and goals also have the purpose to focus the work and attention of everything your group does. Take your time with this task, because every action your non-profit takes in the future or fundraising campaign it runs should be aligned with your defined goals and mission statement.

How To Build A Lasting Foundation For A Non-Profit Organization

After you're able to explain the necessity of your new non-profit, it's time to build a solid foundation, and the strongest foundations start with the founder. If you're the founder... that's you!

According to leadership expert Brian Tracey, who's worked with more than 1,000 organizations, there are five traits that all successful Founders must possess:

1. Self-Discipline: As Brian says best, "If you can discipline yourself to do what you should do, whether you feel like it or not, your success is virtually guaranteed."

2. Integrity: All successful organizations are built on trust. People will be more willing to work with you and support you if they can trust you, especially during difficult times. "Be perfectly honest in everything you do and in every transaction and activity," Brian says. "Never compromise your integrity."

3. Persistence: If you are able to develop a habit of persistence even before you meet obstacles, they will be much easier to get through once you meet them. "The courage to persist in the face of adversity and disappointment is the one quality

that, more than anything, will guarantee your success."

4. A Clear Sense of Direction: In Brian's experience, he's seen motivated entrepreneurs get hijacked by the day-to-day tasks and short-term problems that naturally arise from starting an organization. That's why Brian says to develop a clear sense of direction, not only for your own work but for the people who work with you.

5. Decisive and Action Oriented: Successful founders must think and make decisions quickly. Seek feedback just as quickly and self-correct when needed. Brian says, "The key to triumph is for you to try. Successful people are decisive and they try far more things than other people do."

If you can instill in yourself a strong tie to each of these traits, and live them out in practice, you'll have built the strong foundation your nonprofit needs to succeed in today's world. The next step to start a nonprofit is to develop a clear plan on how your organization will operate.

What To Include In Your Business Plan

Business Plans written with the primary purpose of presenting the company to outsiders differ in format and presentation from a business plan developed as a management tool. While it would benefit the company and management to go through the efforts necessary to establish goals, objectives, strategies and action plans defined near the end of this   chapter, outsiders unfamiliar with not only the company, but also possibly the industry and   products require a different presentation, with an emphasis on selling the reader on the attributes of the company. A plan for strictly internal use is geared more toward defining specific, measurable performance targets and assigns responsibility for reaching those targets.

The business plan document is often the first exposure an investor has to a company seeking to finance, often even before talking to the entrepreneur on the phone or having a meeting. Because it makes the critical "first impression" for the company, a poorly prepared plan can be a reason for an investor to decline on the investment, and not take the time to ask for more information. While we all hear of stories about deals that were scratched out on the back of an envelope, after a brief meeting between a savvy entrepreneur and a multi-millionaire, the truth is: no business plan equals no capital.

1. Describe Your Business/Company:

You have to be very clear about the business that you are in, the exact market that you will be aiming at and how your business is going to be structured. You should mention very quickly the mission of your business in subjective terms as well objective terms using hard figures. Mention details of products, focusing on their benefits to customers and emphasizing on what makes them different from others. In fact, that is the only way your business can grow - if you think of your product and service as something that you're customers and the market needs and wants rather than what you are interested in producing or selling.

2. Talk Up Your Team:

Next, to you, your team is the most important aspect of your business. If you believe that they lend you that special competitive edge, explain why fully giving details of their qualifications and skills as also their industry-related expertise. You will also need to explain what other important job positions you intend to provide and how you are planning on looking for people. And of course, you will also need to emphasize your own qualifications and skills for running this business.

3. Operational Details:

While a broad business plan is good enough to get you started, you will need a detailed operational plan to keep your business going from day to day without any problems.

By including operational details, you will be showing that you have a good grasp of the business requirements and that you have given sufficient thought to the entire production process, reducing the chances for errors and providing for meeting any challenges should one arise. These will include production, distribution, selling and marketing details as also what are the main and alternate sources of supplies. In this increasingly technological age, you should consider and mention how you will effectively use technology to substantially reduce costs and increase productivity.

4. Marketing Plan:

What kind of distribution avenues will your business be using? What methods have you used to decide the pricing of the product, and how do you intend to promote and advertise it? Would you use only traditional modes of distribution and advertising or would you make use of the Internet and e-commerce?

5. Sales Plan:

You will need to include sales projections and revenues and then explain why you are confident that these will come true. Try to defend your expected revenue figures by describing how you plan to convince likely prospects or key distributors to buy. It is important to show that you have given this enough though, that you have ways of convincing retailers and customers to buy your products and also of how your sales team will be working to make this succeed.

6. Risk Assessment:

The most important detail to include in any business plan not only to assure investors that you are working to keep their investment safe and growing but also to make sure that you give enough consideration to all possible risk factors and have plans to mitigate each one of these. You may need to guard against economic downturns, the bankruptcy of a key customer, employee issues and so on. Take nothing for granted.

Your Five Main Sources Of Revenue

How to get money into the non-profit organization is a problem as old as the hills, so don't feel that your situation is unusual. There are four main ways of achieving this:

Donation And Gifts

Donations generally come from individuals (e.g. from a fundraising appeal or given as a legacy), from companies, or from charitable trusts and foundations. Unless they have been given in response to a particular appeal you generally have considerable freedom in how to apply them. Gifts and donations are a particularly important source of income for charities and can attract tax relief. Raising funds, however, can be time-consuming and costly and you could even lose money.

Key issues for members of the charity or non-profit board body to consider.Is your fundraising effective and economic? Have you set cost/income ratios for your fundraising (recognizing that some types of fundraising are more expensive than others) and are you achieving them? Are you claiming back tax (e.g. through Gift Aid)?

Is your fundraising legal? The rules about fundraising can be detailed and complex and you may need to seek advice. There are for example rules on data protection, the use of professional fundraisers, and for house-to-house collections and lotteries.

Is your fundraising ethical? Do you comply with the Institute of Fundraising's Codes of Fundraising Practice? Have you signed up to the self-regulatory scheme for fundraising?

Are your fundraising activities likely to damage your reputation in any way? Do you have policies for example on corporate donations?

Have you made clear what the appeal is for, and what you will do if you raise more or less than the target? Have you ensured that the money will be spent on the purpose for which it was given?

Banks And Other Financial Institutions

When you're thinking of approaching banks and financial institutions remember: Have a decent plan to show them what you are trying to do

They want your business. They have sales targets just like you. If you can put up a decent plan they will fight to get your business.

Don't leave it too late to approach these institutions. There are various different sources of funds from banks

Overdrafts: Never forget that this is a major source of revenue for a bank, and they want your business. Make sure your bank manager knows what's going on and they will be a lot more co-operative.

Lease finance: This enables you to match the costs of buying the asset with the income you generate. However, do read the terms carefully and shop around. Focus on what happens at the end of the lease as there are many options here.

Factoring: Asset-based debts can easily be assigned to a third party. This means they put you in finds immediately and collect the debt for you.

Invoice finance: This is the same thing as factoring, except the customer, does not need to know. This can be very flexible and do whatever you need.

Loans: Again, presented in the right way, this can be an excellent source of finance, particularly as interest rates are so low at the moment. The small firms' loan guarantee scheme may also be helpful in some situations.

Foundation Grants

In a similar category to a government-funded grant, there are also private and public foundations that collect donations and award non-profit organizations grant money based off of a set of criteria or the foundation's stated mission.

There is usually an application and approval process for these awards, sort of a nonprofit version of earning a scholarship. There are a few online database resources that can help you in your search, Foundation Center is particularly useful for its extensive directory and free educational resources.

Government Grants

While this is one funding source that might immediately jump to the forefront of your mind as you consider your options, it's far from the only choice for nonprofits. That said, many organizations do collect at least a part of their budget from this channel. There are several different ways to go about this, but the two most common options are to comply with an existing government program (such as a Head Start) and receive its already allotted funds, or alternatively, there are certain pools of government funds (such as the Prevention and Public Health Fund) that could send money your way if you or your organization is a particularly impactful, innovative, or cost-effective program. With either option, you'll need to reach out and apply. If the sheer volume of grant options seems daunting, the United States government, fortunately, has a searchable online database of government grants to help you find what you need.

For some organizations, government funding is ideal and straightforward. For others, things like meeting the regulations required or negotiating contracts can prove prohibitive. You will want to do your research and make sure that applying for government grants is in the best interest of your mission.

Corporate Sponsorship

Seek connections with corporate sponsors. Whether it's a monetary donation or donating the use of space for an event, this type of arrangement is a win-win. You get to meet some of your organization's needs, and the company sponsors improve their philanthropic image within the community. Different corporations will have different giving programs, this list of types of corporate funding options is helpful as you familiarize yourself with the possibilities that may work for your organization.

Many for-profit groups see giving back to their communities as a vital part of their mission, and as long as you accept donations from socially responsible corporations that are aligned with the goals and values of your nonprofit work, this can be a valuable strategic partnership. Some organizations may feel a little apprehensive about receiving funding from a for-profit corporation, and while this can be a very beneficial route, it is important to carefully screen your corporate funding sources.

How To Choose The Best Name For Your Non-Profit

A lot depends on the name of your non-profit organization and even on what you call your projects and programs.

Will your name become a household word? Will it quickly and eloquently convey what you do? Or will it be a made-up word that means nothing, a name that bores everyone or a hodge-podge of terms that only insiders in your field understand?

Many organizations spend thousands of dollars on research to determine what to name themselves. Or they hire expensive consultants who may not even understand your audience, much less your mission.

But, a group of people with common sense can often brainstorm names and come up with winners.

Tips On Choosing The Best Name

Use descriptive words.

A strong name should embody the mission of your organization. But be careful. Simply calling your organization The Coalition to Stop Violence against Children (made that up, but it probably exists) may be a very descriptive name, but it lacks emotion, isn't that inspiring and is rather long. A descriptive name should have an emotional impact.

Make sure it is easy to spell, make an acronym. This is a common technique and very effective if done well. How about a non-profit that mentors inner-city schools with local business leaders called, "Business and Education Succeeding Together" or B.E.S.T. Acronyms don't have to spell anything either. NPR, NAACP, and AARP are some very well- known examples of this. But be careful, acronyms don't often spell a word or describe your mission. So be sure to include your tagline or the full spelling of your name in your published materials.

Test Your Name

Once you have some ideas for your name you should run them through a few test. Pretend you are answering the phone in your organization's office. How does it sound? Do you feel awkward saying it? What is your emotional response when you hear it out loud? Does it sound too corporate, stiff, silly, serious or jingly?

Does the name leave your options to grow? For instance, what if the Cleveland River Cleanup Corp wanted to expand into other parts of the state?

Test your name out on your friends. Ask them which they like and why. Did one name sound more inspiring? Is one easier to remember?

Legal Considerations

Many states require that non-profits have a corporate designator, such as Incorporated, Corporation, Company, Limited or their abbreviations (Inc., Corp., Co., and Ltd respectively). Check your state's incorporation web page to see if a corporate designator is required for your nonprofit.

Some Final Checks

Now that you have selected your name you need to check with your Secretary of State to see if it is available. Visit the State Non-profit Links map on this website to find this database.

It's also advisable to do some other name checks depending on the plans for your non- profit:

If you plan to have offices in another state then check that state's database as well.

Check the U.S. Department of Commerce website to be sure the name you want is not trademarked.

See if the domain for your non-profit name is available. This may or may not affect your decision to use the name, but if the domain is already taken, it is good to know what type of content is on that site.

If your domain is taken, but you really want to use the name, you can try adding your states name to the domain or add "inc" to the end of the domain name or put "the" at the beginning of the domain name. Also, remember, non-profits should be .org not .com.

Be sure that your name is not similar to another organizations name. This may be technically legal to do in some cases, but people may think that your organization is a branch of the other. In general, it is best to have a unique name for your organization.

How To Recruit Your Board

Start by asking what does your non-profit need to advance its mission right now and in the future? A board member with financial expertise? Connections in the community? Someone familiar with the individuals served by the nonprofit? Once you have identified the skills and experience your nonprofit needs, you're ready to identify and recruit new board members. The recruitment process requires both "vetting" a candidate and "cultivating" the interest of a potential future board member until he or she is ready to accept an invitation to become an ambassador and advocate for the nonprofit. Some nonprofits find that asking potential board candidates to first serve on a committee or task force, or volunteer for the nonprofit in another way, is a good way for both nonprofit and potential board member to find a good fit.

"Nominating committee" implies that the only function is to nominate board members for election to the board, but that limits our vision of good governance. It's helpful to have a task force or committee of the board authorized not only to identify new board prospects but also to focus on the effectiveness of the board. Serving on a charitable nonprofit's board is about more than just being elected – it requires continuous learning about those served and being an advocate for the mission, making decisions that are in the best interest of the organization, ensuring prudent use of the nonprofit's assets, and looking ahead to help the nonprofit plan for the future. All this requires "the vision thing," which is bolstered by ongoing education and exposure to issues that affect the nonprofit's operations – both its external and internal environments.

As the name "Governance Committee" suggests, the focus of what used to be called the "nominating committee" is now on effective board governance, and its role goes well beyond nominating. The committee tasked with keeping the board on track is usually also responsible for ensuring that the nonprofit has effective governance practices, that individual board members are engaged, and that the board as a whole is effectively fulfilling its obligations as a steward of the nonprofit's assets, reputation, financial and human resources, and mission.

Strategy To Recruit Your Board.

1. Post your "Great Board Member Wanted" ad on free websites that match people seeking boards to join with non-profits seeking board members. We like:

www.boardnetusa.org for its national (if uneven) reach, the info it collects, and the other resources there

www.volunteermatch.org for its very wide distribution, although it's much better known for referring program volunteers than for board volunteers

www.bridgestar.org uses the boardnetusa.org database, but adds individuals from its (mostly corporate) members, and has good additional resources for board members less familiar with the nonprofit sector

2. Place a "Help Wanted--Volunteer Board Member" ad on your lobby bulletin board, in your newsletter, in the neighborhood newspaper, or in the alumni newsletter of a local college. Example: "HELP SOUTH PARK... We're looking for a few talented and conscientious volunteer board members to lead and strengthen our programs for people with Alzheimer's and their families. If you can contribute your time, thoughtfulness, and leadership one evening a month, and are interested in exploring this opportunity, call John at xxx-xxx to find out whether this volunteer opportunity is right for you. We're especially looking for folks with accounting experience, with gerontology backgrounds, from the Asian communities, or who are on the younger side of the community.

3. Our best idea: Form a "One Hour Recruiting Task Force." Draw up a list of twenty well- connected people of the sort you would want on the board but who you suspect wouldn't join, (but who might know someone who would be a good board member.) Call those twenty people and ask them

to come to one meeting of the Task Force committee over lunch (confess it will actually take an hour-and-a-half). Tell them that at the lunch they'll be told more about the organization and what it's looking for in board members.

At the end of lunch, they'll be asked simply for the name of one person they think would be a good board member. The Task Force is disbanded. The day after the lunch call up each of the nominees and begin by explaining who nominated them.

4. Promote through the ranks: Ask the executive director or the volunteer coordinator if there are two or three hands-on volunteers who would make good board members. Hands- on volunteers, such as support group facilitators, practical life support volunteers, volunteer ushers, weekend tree-planters, classroom aides and others bring both demonstrated commitment AND an intimate knowledge of the organization's strengths and weaknesses. Volunteers, donors, and clients should be the first place you look. You don't have to "sell" the agency - they know it already!

5. Board Member Swap: Pick four local organizations where you don't know anyone, but you'd like to (examples: NAACP, Japanese American Citizens League, Accountants for the Public Interest, community hospital). (Tip: Your local Yahoo site (http://www.yahoo.com/) is a good place to look for lists under "Community.") Ask each officer to call one of the four local organizations and ask to have coffee with one of their leaders. Over coffee suggest that your two organizations recommend "retiring" board members to each other as a way of establishing organizational links and strengthening ties among communities.

Filing For Tax-Exemption

There are several types of businesses that are eligible to apply for tax exemptions from the government. These business types include churches, charities, political organizations, private charitable foundations and other non-profit business types. There are very specific IRS requirements and regulations in place for tax-exempt organizations, which must be followed closely in order to retain the exemption each year. Keep in mind that attaining tax-exempt status with the IRS is for federal taxes only.

State tax exemptions are handled on the state level and may have different qualifications and requirements.

Applying For Tax Exempt Status

In order to apply for tax exemption, a business must follow the process lined out by the Internal Revenue Service. An Employer Identification Number must be obtained before applying for an exemption, even if an organization has no employees. This can be done online, over the phone or by filing a form SS-4 either by mail or by fax.

Once an EIN has been issued, the organization can then apply for recognition as a tax- exempt business from the IRS by filing Form 1023 or Package 1024. Be sure to fill out the form completely and accurately in order to have your application processed in a timely manner. According to the IRS, the factor causing the most delays in processing exemption applications is businesses failing to submit the correct user fee for the application. Refer to section 6 of the current Revenue Procedure guide to find the correct fee.

Now you can hold your organization's first formal board meeting to document the fact that you have officially kicked off your new nonprofit corporation. At this meeting, you should elect the officers of your organization and designate to open the necessary bank accounts as you will need this resolution in order to do so.

And, now you have arrived! You are now at the final step in becoming a tax-exempt charitable organization by applying for your tax exemption from the Internal Revenue Service. In order to do so, you must request what is known as a determination letter or rule from the IRS. This is the official IRS letter stating that it has determined that your organization qualifies as a tax-exempt organization under the applicable sections of the IRS code. You request tax-exempt status by submitting to the IRS the Application of Recognition of Exemption or IRS Form 1023 which can be downloaded from the IRS website.

Regulations for Tax Exempt Organizations

There are many regulations that govern tax-exempt organizations, set out by the IRS. These must be followed in order to retain a tax-exempt status. Specific rules about where and how funds are obtained, lobbying taxes and allowed programs are of the utmost importance. Failure to adhere to the regulations governing tax-exempt organizations will result in the loss of the status. The requirements vary depending on the company's status as a public charity or private organization, so each organization should be sure that they are following the correct guidelines, as given by the IRS in various publications.

Organizational Test

The stated purpose of the nonprofit organization must be exclusively for one or more of the exempt purposes described in section 501(c) (3). The purpose must be included in the nonprofit's governing documents (such as the Articles of Incorporation) with the correct wording to meet certain IRS requirements. The two primary concerns for passing the organizational test is that the purpose is clearly limited to the options within the 501(c)(3) section and that the assets of the organization are irrevocably dedicated to one or more exempt purposes.

Operational Test

The actual operations of the organization must be primarily dedicated to the stated exempt purposes. Although the regulation uses the term exclusively, in that the organization must be operated exclusively for one or more of the exempt purposes set forth in section 501(c)(3), in fact, the organization can allow an "insubstantial part" of its activities to be geared to non-exempt purposes, such as operating an unrelated business. However, the profits from that unrelated, non-exempt purpose may be subject to business taxes. But from a standpoint of qualifying for

501(c)(3) status, the organization should be operated primarily for the stated exempt purposes.

No Private Inurement

Private inurement occurs when an individual who has a good bit of influence over an organization receives benefits greater than what they put in. Nonprofits with 501(c)(3) status are absolutely prohibited from allowing its assets to personally benefit any insider, including board members, officers, and key employees. Any incident of "excess benefit transactions" like overcompensating an insider can lead to revocation of the organization's exempt status or financial sanctions (excise taxes) imposed by the IRS. It is critical to set up policies that eliminate the temptation for insiders to take advantage of their involvement in the organization and to police the transactions that do occur within the nonprofit.

No Substantial Lobbying

The 501(c) (3) regulations prohibit qualifying organizations from participating in lobbying as a substantial portion of their activities. Lobbying, or attempting to influence legislation in any way, is allowed to some degree, but it cannot be a primary focus of the nonprofit. Also, there is a difference between lobbying and merely being involved in public policy. Lobbying is defined as advocating for or against, or contacting, or urging the public to contact, members or employees of a legislative body (Congress, state legislature, local councils, and the like) for the purpose of proposing, supporting, or opposing the legislation. Activities such as distributing educational materials or hosting educational meetings about public policy issues are allowed and will not jeopardize the organization's tax-exempt status.

No Political Campaigning

Section 501(c) (3) also prohibits organizations from participating in the support or opposition of any political candidate. Donating funds to a campaign and making public statements for or against a political candidate risks the revocation of the nonprofit's exempt status and subjects the organization to financial sanctions.

However, 501(c)(3)s are allowed to participate in the electoral process as nonpartisan players, such as providing voter education and encouraging voter registration, as long as there is no indication of support or opposition for any side of the election.

These five factors are the foundation of qualifying for 501(c) (3) status, and thus providing a nonprofit organization tax-exemption and the potential for donors to deduct their contributions. It is critical for all nonprofit founders to understand and adhere to each of these in order to protect the benefits that come with 501(c) (3) status.

Filing Obligations for Tax-Exempt Organizations

Although these organizations may be exempt from paying certain federal taxes, financial information must be submitted to the IRS each year, in most cases. Depending on the income of the organization, they will need Form 990, 990-T, 990-EZ or 990-N. There are some organizations, such as churches, religious organizations and government-run organizations that do not have to file any additional forms. Other forms may be required if a tax-exempt organization has paid employees or if there is taxable income from certain sources within the fiscal year

CHAPTER FOUR:
Setting Up You Non-Profit Office

When you begin to set up your non-profit office, one of two things tends to happen. Either you are unable to easily identify what equipment and technology you use every day so you underestimate what you will need to get your office up and running, and quickly find yourself struggling. Or, you clearly see each individual item you may need and are overwhelmed by the thought of meeting every one of those needs down to the last staple.

In either of these cases, it wouldn't be a surprise to find yourself running around in circles before you're able to focus your efforts and create an office that will help you work productively.

Use this checklist to develop a well-rounded yet streamlined list of what you need in your home office. Check the items you absolutely need and circle the items you may eventually want to add to create a prioritized list of your home office essentials.

Step 1: Make A List of Everything You need For Your Office

Make a list of everything you will need in your new office, from desks and chairs to computer hardware, as well as any tasks like setting up your internet connection.

Common Office Needs

Desks: Options for any layout or working style

Ideally, you will have space for a traditional desk where you create an ergonomically correct workstation. But, if you need to get creative, you can make a table, counter or other flat surface work.

Chairs

Best office chairs for any budget. Take time to select and invest in a comfortable chair; it is one of the most important parts of an efficient home office. Again, ergonomics and comfort count when it comes to sitting, so make sure you test out a chair before making a purchase.

Computers: Choosing desktop vs. laptop, Mac or PC

You clearly need a monitor if you have a desktop computer, but it can also be useful (and better for your neck) to have a monitor you plug into your laptop. Depending on the work you do, you may also consider dual monitors.

Phone Service: Recommendations for VoIP phone service

With VoIP technology, Internet-based phone services, and even mobile phones, you may not need a traditional landline telephone, but access to a phone service is usually necessary for non- profit organization.

Desk Phones Reviews of the best VoIP phones for any office

Not always required, a network router can be necessary if you have more than one computer that needs Internet access. Consider a wireless router if you have a laptop and computers located in different parts of your home.

Internet Service: Recommendations for fast internet providers

Not always required, a network router can be necessary if you have more than one computer that needs Internet access. Consider a wireless router if you have a laptop and computers located in different parts of your home.

An Easier Option for Office Phones

Save time to choose office phones and a phone service. Search for service that offers high- quality phone service using your existing internet connection, with all of the features you need, for half the price of traditional landlines.

Adequate Lighting

Just as a good chair is important for an ergonomic home office, so is having adequate lighting levels. You don't want to deal with headaches and eye strain from squinting or using lighting that makes it hard to read.

Software

Some non-profit owners simply need access to word processing, spreadsheet, and email management applications, while others need additional software that is specific to their needs. Make a list of the software you will need to run your home office.

Printer/Multipurpose Machine

If you have a paperless office, you may be able to get away without having a printer, but there may be situations when you need to scan, fax and even make copies. If this is common in your business, look into multipurpose machines that can manage all of these tasks.

File Cabinet

Even if you aim to be paperless, there are always some hard copy documents you need to hang on to. The best place to store these documents and be able to find them later is in a file cabinet.

Uninterruptible Power Supply (UPS)

A UPS provides backup power for a limited time in case your electricity goes out because UPS can provide you with useful buffer time to save your work and safely shut down your equipment.

Backup Drive/Personal Server

Once your office is up and running, you will need to have a plan for backing up and protecting your data. You can use cloud-based backup services to copy your files automatically, but it is also a good idea to consider having an in-house backup in place. External drives and personal servers are relatively affordable and can save your business in the case of computer failure.

Paper Shredder

A shredder is a must for destroying sensitive and confidential information in your business. And for every other piece of non-sensitive paper, consider getting a recycling bin.

There will certainly be other items you need in your home office, depending on the type of work you do and how much you space have available. But if you use this checklist to get started thinking about the essentials, you are on your way to creating a streamlined and efficient home office.

Fire-Safe Box

Speaking of storage, you may consider using a fire-safe box to store and protect your most important paperwork. Many small business owners also use these durable boxes to keep backup copies of their data.

Optional Office Needs

Alarm System: Compare the pros and cons of personal and professional systems

Insurance: A CGL policy can cover accidents, like a slip and fall in your office. To cover office property damage, however, you'll need commercial property insurance

Phone Answering Service: If you want a live agent answering your phone, but can't afford a full-time receptionist, check out our full guide to answering services

General Office Supplies For everything else (and then some), there's Amazon.

Step 2: Design You Office Floor Plan

Once you have a list of everything you will need, the next step is to lay it out. This will also help you to confirm how much furniture you will need to buy. First, start by choosing a layout type:

An open plan maximizes the usable area of the space, but at the expense of privacy and storage.

A closed plan gives your staff more personal space, but it's less collaborative and won't fit as many seats

A modular plan combines elements of both, giving your staff more privacy, storage, and larger working surfaces but with open areas between seats for collaboration

You can use simple blueprint software, such as Edraw (locally installed) or Smart Draw (cloud-based), to drag-and-drop workstations, desks, and other items to help you design your office space.

Step 3: Set Up Ypour Phone System

You have several options when choosing which phone system is best for your business. Some of these include:

Traditional phone service, which runs on old copper phone lines

VoIP phone service, which transmits voice as data over your internet connection .

Virtual phone service, which forwards calls made to your business phone number to your personal phone line

VoIP phone service is a great option for most businesses since it is more affordable than a landline and just as clear. You can also easily add or subtract as many lines as you need, and you'll be able to get phone service within minutes of plugging in your phone.

Another useful feature that most providers include is an auto-attendant, which automatically answers your incoming calls and presents your callers with a list of options to choose from. Depending on which option the caller chooses, their call will be routed according to the call tree you set up.

Auto-attendants can be set up with the VoIP phone service in your office or with a virtual phone service. The only difference is where it routes your calls. With a VoIP phone service, the call will be routed to the appropriate phone on the office's network; with a virtual phone service, the call will be forwarded to the appropriate personal phone line you've defined.

Step 4: Find The Best Furniture & Computers

Next, choose the best office furniture and computers for your business' needs and budget.

Office Desks

Which office desks you choose will largely depend on your office layout.

With an open plan, simple rectangular tables that you can group together will usually work the best. When we first started out at Fit Small Business, we used simple folding tables like this one. This gave us a quick, inexpensive, and flexible solution that we could easily rearrange into any layout. The downside to folding tables is they don't allow any room for storage, nor are they the particularly stylish.

For a little more money, you can buy glass, metal, or faux wood tables that usually include some storage options in their design. L-shaped tables, in particular, are great for setting up a modular plan.

Office Chairs

While there are many low-priced office chairs on the market, we recommend buying the best your budget can afford. Good chairs help to promote a happy and healthy work environment — your staff is spending most of their day on them, so investing in their comfort shows them that you value them. You might also be saving money on lost productivity — several of us at Fit Small Business have experienced great improvements in back pain after upgrading our office chairs.

Office Computers

If you're going to be providing the same, or similar, computers to your whole staff rather than letting them choose their own, the first decision you will need to make is what type of computer to buy. Desktop computers generally provide better value with more storage and better performance, but laptop computers are more portable.

Then, you will need to choose which operating system to work on:

Apple OS X is ideal for graphics, video, and audio editing and desktop publishing

Chrome books are an inexpensive option if your business will primarily be using the Google suite and other web-based software

Windows, which is a widely-used and flexible platform.

Step 5: Set up Internet

Although we've listed it as the fourth step, you should be researching which internet service provider (ISP) to connect your office with well before you move in. Before committing to any office lease, make sure the location is serviceable by a high-speed internet provider. You can confirm this by searching the FCC's National Broadband Map.

Then, once you've found a few providers, compare their plans, prices, and contracts. Also, remember that commercial accounts often differ from residential ones, so be careful when looking at their terms.

For most small businesses, an internet connection with a minimum of 15 Mbps download and 5 Mbps will be sufficient. However, as file sizes become larger and more content is being streamed on the internet, the faster the connection the better. We recommend 50 Mbps download and 10 Mbps upload connections if they're available.

Hiring Your Staffs

No matter the size, every non-profit must build a strong team in order to be successful. I have had the privilege of being on the selection committee for hiring four new executive directors for various non-profits over the last several years. In all but one of the cases we used the process you'll find below. The best part of this process is that it has stood the test of time and has been enhanced by technology. Here is my five-step process to a successful non-profit team hire:

1. Cast a Wide Net

The first step is to cast as wide of a internet as possible searching for potential candidates. The larger the pool of candidates, the greater the chance you have of finding a truly special person. Think in terms of PR and social media: networking and communications are key elements. The hidden secret is to never stop the process! Keep networking and your list of potential team members will grow.

2. Email Open-Ended Questions

The ability to write is a vital skill in just about every single role associated with a non- profit. It is also an easy manner to whittle down whatever size pool of candidates you have assembled. My preference here is to email out a list of ten open-ended questions to every candidate after your initial communications following an inquiry into the position.

Make sure you write questions that: Are fun to answer.
Require no or little research

Allows the candidate's personality to shine through
Allows you to see their writing skills
Have a short deadline for completion

It is best to let them ask you 1-2 questions back. By limiting the number they can ask, you make your review easier and it forces the candidates to be insightful. Be sure and note how many of the candidates meet or beat the deadline as that is a superb indicator of their future ability to do so.

This step should allow you to reduce the pool of candidates down to 4-8 who move on to the next step. If possible, use 2 or more existing team members to help select those who move on to the next step.

3. Short Telephone Interview

Next, schedule a 20-30 minute phone interview with your leading candidates. Your goal is to not only find out more about them but also to see how they handle themselves over the phone. Have the same 10-15 questions prepared for all candidates, and be prepared to write or type their answers so you can review them later. In addition, you should write your impressions of the candidate right after the call while they're fresh in your mind.

The nature and type of questions are key to insights gained and comparisons garnered. Here are some suggestions to help:

Ask questions that place the candidate in situations they will be facing and ask what they will do.

For any action or decision they talk about always ask why (you need to know how they think and process).

Avoid resume related questions (the candidates are used to answering those!) Ask questions that uncover their inner values and amount of work ethic.

In the beginning, inform them they will be able to ask you up to three questions toward the end. Note exactly what 2-3 questions they ask and how insightful they are (huge differentiator) We always make sure 2-3 people conduct the telephone interviews thus providing your team with multiple opinions and rating sheets to compare. Once all the interviews are completed and the rating sheets reviewed, pick the three finalists to move to ensuing step.

4. Face-to-Face Interview

By now, you have established their writing skills, telephone communication skills, the type of thinking they exhibit through their answers to your open-ended questions and the types of questions they ask you.Now, it's time for a face-to-face interview.

This step should provide the finalists a chance to meet multiple members of your team and to experience your organization's environment.

Here are some key parameters to keep in mind for the face-to-face interviews:

If possible, have the candidates come on separate consecutive days

Have them interview with at least four or more members of your team

Use a mix of one-on-one and group interviews (this allows more note taking)

Use as many "situational" experience and action questions (you want to know their internal values and method of making decisions)

Have a few questions that allow you to see if the candidate will fit into and/or enhance your culture

Do your background checks, particularly social media information beforehand, if possible, so you can ask questions that might help explain items (be careful to not ask improper questions from HR perspective)

Make sure at least one of your questions explores compensation and future evaluation criteria

As before, have the questions written down so the same questions are used for each candidate

Write down all answers during the interview, as well as your opinion right at the completion of the interview

All of the interviewers should gather as soon as possible after the interview sessions end to compare evaluations. The top two should remain for the last step, but keep the third person ready should one or both of the finalists not work out.

5. Leadership Presentation or Immersion

Here, choose between either a presentation to leadership or immersion.

The leadership presentation is designed for your team to see first-hand the finalist's talents in the following areas:

Researching and creating a 90-day to 1-year game plan
Presenting the plan in a group setting with only a whiteboard
Inspiring the group reviewing the plan

Answering questions on the fly
Challenge the candidate to pull together the details of a game plan for their new role and present the details without handouts or slides. They must work from a whiteboard using only their words and gestures.

Whereas a leadership presentation is ideal for those applying for a leadership role, immersion is ideal for a non-leadership role. These finalists spend either a half day (or preferably a full day) shadowing current team members and performing or interacting with other team members in the same role.

The goal of this exercise is to provide a real life, long-term view of what the job and the environment entail and requires. It also helps eliminate surprises later. Both the finalists and the other team members have a chance to see if it feels right.

For both options, the team members involved should huddle to review all the information from the original email questions to the final step. This is bringing many of the new team member's future peers into the process, which pays many long-term dividends! In most cases, a clear winner will emerge due to the completeness of the process. This process helps ensure only the best fitting and most top-notch candidate is added to the team.

It's Not Just for Your Internal Staff

Keep in mind, various portions and variations of this process can be used for selecting board members, recruiting volunteers, finding partners and choosing consultants or vendors. There's no reason why those individuals shouldn't be as involved and committed as yourself or your top employees. Just imagine a board meeting where every board member:

Wanted to be there

Understood the mission and the means of the NPO fully Communicated well

Desired to be involved beyond the actual board meeting

Providing positive influence on introducing others to your organization Sounds like a slice of heaven, doesn't it?

Finding the best staff of any type can make such a difference for any organization moving forward! Pick and choose what best fits your organization and its needs for the future. Now you have five concrete steps which allow you to do just that. Best of luck in building your team!

How To Start a Non- Profit Revenue Plan

No nonprofit I've come across has figured out how to do all four exceptionally well. While some do well with donations, others do better with grants, etc. But, what I have seen work best when approaching all four at once is to have separate strategies for each different revenue source. Below I'll cover the basics of each revenue source and how to develop a strategy for your nonprofit.

How to Get Funding For Your Nonprofit

It is the burning question of every non-profit organization: "How do we get funding?" With the economy in the dumps and recovery looks like a distant hope, this question screams for an answer. In fact, we get more requests from newsletter subscribers on funding than just about any other topic. The purpose of this is to do just that, but maybe not like you expect.

So, what does it take to get funding? Let's look at several, key concepts.

Purpose. First and foremost, your organization must have a compelling purpose…one that resonates with the public, or at least with a segment of the public that shares your passion. Without this, you simply will not attract dollars. There is a persistent and, frankly, bizarre notion in the nonprofit community of "Build it and they will come." That is especially true regarding the pursuit of grant funding. Well, that may work well in baseball movies, but not so much in the charity community. Your organization is one of literally millions of projects that are competing for someone's charitable dollar. You can conduct all the cake walks you want, but if no one cares about your cause, funding is not on its way. Many of you reading this are probably saying, "Well, that's not very helpful. We're already forced to do what we do." That's true…and we're not saying you should change your purpose to something more attractive. The point is this: If your purpose is therapeutic arts for handicapped kids, then your ability to attract a broad base of support is many times greater than if your purpose is to operate an injured skunk rescue. If yours is the injured skunk rescue, then you need to be realistic about your lack of mass appeal and be extra aggressive in finding like-minded donors.

Vision. People give to vision, not need. They sound the same, but they are not. Vision paints a picture of a better situation that results from your organization's efforts. Need, on the other hand…well, right now everyone has needs. Paint a picture instead.

Accomplishments. Nothing attracts people like a winner. What has your organization accomplished? Let people know about it. That is really true when pursuing grant opportunities. People are not as likely to give to plans as they are to helping you do more of what you've already done. If you are just starting out, you better concentrate on #2!

Reliability. You must be able to show your potential donors that your organization is properly structured, has good governance and that it is operating in compliance with governmental regulations. If not, you will have difficulty projecting a posture of trustworthiness. If people do not have confidence that their donations are going to be used wisely, and by an organization who takes things seriously enough to follow the rules, they will not give. Period.

Motivated leadership. It all starts at the top. If those who are leading the organization are not fully engaged, why should anyone want to support your efforts? This concept goes back to a point we've made in prior chapters: never, ever have a "placeholder" board. Make sure your board members are motivated leaders who care about the mission and who have something to contribute. And by contribute, we mean time, talent and money…all three. People look to see if the leadership walks the walk, or just talks the talk.

Dogged determination. This is important at all times. In bad times, it simply means life or death to your organization. Determine to succeed. Stay motivated. It's contagious. You cannot give up. Our staff could tell you story after story of clients we've worked with who, by all outward appearances, couldn't find their way out of a wet paper bag, much less succeed in running a nonprofit. But they have. By sheer force of determination and belief in their cause, and by surrounding themselves with competent help, they made it happen. We've also seen the opposite: people who should've hit a home run, only to strike out because of neglecting one or more of these issues.

We're all about building foundations. It's in our name. We hope by helping you see the big picture, you'll be in a much better position to work on developing specific funding ideas that will work.

No nonprofit I've come across has figured out how to do all four exceptionally well. While some do well with donations, others do better with grants, etc. But, what I have seen work best when approaching all four at once is to have separate strategies for each different revenue source. Below I'll cover the basics of each revenue source and how to develop a strategy for your non-profit.

How To Start a Non-Profit Revenue Stream

Revenue from goods and services include money made from membership dues, event tickets, professional services, and products like merchandise. For example, the writing association I'm a member of charges a yearly membership fee, event ticket fees, fees for professional editing, and they sell t-shirts.

The two biggest contributors in this form of revenue are from membership dues and event tickets, which I cover below.

Membership Dues

Membership dues are the monthly or yearly price people pay to become a member of your organization. But, people will only join your nonprofit if there's something in it for them. A study of over 800 associations reveals the two main reasons anyone joins an association (this also applies to other types of nonprofits):

Access to a unique community of like-minded individuals.

Nothing engages and attracts members greater than the desire to belong to a community who shares their personal interests. And among the most popular ways to build a community of like-minded individuals is through networking events. In fact, here's an example of an association who grew over 1,000 members just by attracting new people to network at their annual conference.

1) Access to specialized information and resources in your niche

What can your organization offer that someone would actually pay for? Imagine you've started a Writing Association. The types of specialized information you can offer could look like this (in fact, these are some of the specific reasons I joined my Writing Association):

- Writing workshops
- Education sessions on how to pitch a novel to agents
- Legal advice when it comes to copywriting

How to create a community people want to be a part of and resources people can't wait to access.

People join communities and access resources because they create value. Unfortunately, creating value is one of the biggest struggles of new nonprofits.

"Why aren't people coming to my events? Why aren't people asking to use our services?" These are questions I hear all the time. The reason is that holding the right types of events and creating the right types of resources takes a lot of understanding and hard work. You need to know who exactly to attract and what exactly they're looking for. Surprisingly, this is actually where the for-profit world can lend a hand. For-profit businesses don't have grants, donations, and dues to rely on for revenue, so they must figure out how to create enough value for their products and services to generate profit.

To create value, for-profit businesses follow five steps, which can easily be applied to any nonprofit strategy. Here are those 5 steps as offered from Inc.com, which I've tailored to a nonprofit standpoint:

Step 1: Understand what drives value for your members
The only way to understand what drives your members is to talk directly to member prospects and find out what kind

of information, events, and services they would be willing to pay for.

Step 2: Understand your value proposition

Having a clear and concise value proposition is the easiest way to interest a prospective member in your organization. As Word stream explains, "A value proposition tells prospects why they should do business with you rather than your competitors, and makes the benefits of your products or services crystal clear from the outset." Or, in nonprofit terms — "Why should someone become a member and what promise are you offering them in return." But, a successful value proposition is more than just words, it's the look and feel of your brand, your website, your services, your events, and how you treat members.

Take for instance the Apple iPhone. Wordsteam suggests that the Apple iPhone experience IS the product. Anyone who owns an iPhone can tell you how simple the interface is, how beautiful the design is, and how easy (and addicting) it is to use. In the same way, what value proposition are you offering prospective members that will want them to join your organization? Imagine you're a tennis club. What makes you stand out from the other tennis club down the street? When a prospective member visits your tennis club, what's the impression of the courts, equipment, change rooms, etc.?

Step 3: Identify the members who you are able to create the most value possible for

The most successful nonprofits create profiles of their ideal members so they know where to find these people, how to talk to them, and their needs. It's because they know these ideal members so well that they can offer them exactly what they want. Ideal members are also referred to as a Target Market. "Nonprofits are as passionate about serving as many people as possible, they tend to think wide versus deep," says Susan Burn ash, Nonprofit Marketing Strategist. "They would rather say 'We serve homeless people,' than 'we service homeless senior adults in the city of Atlanta.' Although this is admirable from an organizational standpoint to have such a philanthropic mission, from a marketing perspective, this blanket statement (and Target Market) is a marketing disaster waiting to happen." Susan also suggests some questions you can answer to help you create your own Target Market:

- Who would join your organization?
- What are their age and gender? What are their interests? What is their income level?
- Where do these people live? Where do they hang out? Where do they get their news from?

Once you have your Target Market identified, you'll have a much better idea of what products and services to offer and how to advertise them to these people.

Step 4: Create a win-win price

The price you charge members to join your organization is called a member due. Member dues are often paid on a monthly or yearly basis, and quite often nonprofits make their member dues renew automatically monthly after month or year after year until a member cancels their membership (this saves a lot of time in administration).

While there is no perfect formula for determining your member due to price, your goal is to create a win-win scenario:

A win for your members that keeps member dues low.

A win for your organization that covers as many administrative costs as possible through member dues.

With some basic math, you can figure out how much revenue you can expect from your organization from member dues:

Expected Members x Yearly Member Dues = Yearly Revenue

Ex. 500 Members x $50 Yearly Member Dues = $25,000 Yearly Revenue

In the above example, $25,000 is certainly not enough to run an entire organization and pay staff. That's where event fees, donations, grants, and products and services also contribute. But before you jump to other sources of revenue, there's one more step to ensure you build a robust member-due driven revenue stream.

Step 5: Focus investments on your most valuable members

Which do you expect to be more valuable to your organization in the long run?

1. One new member?
2. One retained member?

The answer is definitely one retained member. That's because the costs of finding and convincing a new member to join your organization can be up to 25 times more expensive than keeping a current member engaged. So, when creating value to attract members, consider how you will retain them in the long run. As time goes by, you may have to refresh your strategy to keep up with the times. To help you out, here are 12 practical ways to engage and retain member in today's world.

Event Fees

I know a Lawyer's Association that runs completely off event fees without charging membership dues. That's because they've created a regular schedule of amazing events that sell out every time.

However, this isn't the case with most organizations who use events as a tool to supplement their revenue and to attract new members.

How much you rely on events for revenue depends on what type of organization you're starting (a tennis club, vs a foundation, would have drastically different event revenue). However, to help you see what most nonprofits do when it comes to events, I analyzed over 1,000,000 events created nonprofit customers.

CHAPTER FIVE:
Fundraising for Non-Profit Organization

Fundraising for a non-profit organization is a big task. Once you have started a non-profit organization you need lots of money to run it smoothly. Though there will be board members who are involved in the organization you need money to achieve your goals. Asking for donations or appealing for donations to the general public will generate some money but if you really want to organize fundraising for non-profit organizations you need to put in lots of work.

The first step in conducting fundraising for a non-profit organization is the planning. You need to plan for everything that needs to be done. You need to first identify the object. Why do you need the money? How much is it going to cost you? How are you going to use the money that you collect? How much money you have to spend in order to raise enough money. The aspect of the human resource, how many people will you need to organize a successful fundraiser?

Once you have all the answers to the questions the eve of fundraising for non-profit organizations becomes less difficult. After you decide to go for fundraising you need to do some research on the market. You need to advertise the event. Send out flyers and emails to prospective donors. Make sure that the event gets maximum publicity. There are people in the society who are willing to donate the money but they need to be informed about you and your needs.

Another important thing that you need to keep in mind is how often you will need to raise funds. It is going to be an ongoing activity or is it going to be an annual event. Within depth market research and careful planning of the activities, the picture should be clear.

If you have a ready plan of activities and the goals you want to achieve for about three to five years raising the money and having enough money to achieve your set goals will be easy. If everything is documented then it will help you in deciding what worked and what didn't. It will also show you where you can cut the cost and how many volunteers you need for such an event.

Once you know the goal you can look for various options open for you. There are some charitable organizations or family trusts who can give you some money for your cause. You need to identify them. You also should have a list of probable donors who are interested in doing some charity work or whose name would be beneficial to your organization if you can get the celebrity to endorse the event.

There are various ways to organize a fundraising for non-profit organizations. Throwing a party for a cause can attract many people who want to have a good time and do their bit for the society as well. Or if the goal is something to do for the education of lesser fortunate kids then you could organize a cake and pie fundraiser should work.

Fundraising Idea

Are you looking for fundraising ideas for non-profit organizations? There are thousands of different fundraisers you can try today! It does not matter if you are looking to raise money for your local sports team, the cheerleading squad, the local church, youth group, or other charity organization. There are probably thousands of different fundraiser programs available today! It is easy to get overwhelmed with all of the different ideas that are out there! Some fundraisers work better than others, so you want to make sure you pick the best fundraising program to fit your group's needs.

When you are coming up with fundraising ideas for non-profit organizations, the biggest challenge is finding a program that your group will be excited to sell. The second biggest challenge is finding programs that sell well too. We must be honest with ourselves when it comes to raising money. Most people don't like selling, and most people aren't just going to buy because it is for a good cause. If you pick the wrong product, it could mean the difference in losing thousands of dollars in funds! For this reason, you should pick products that will appeal to the most people.

One of the fundraising ideas for non-profit organizations that are not effective today is magazine fundraisers. The digital age has sparked a surge in freely flowing information. If you want to know about the latest celebrity gossip, most people head to the internet. If you want to know what is happening in sports, you head to the sports websites. Magazines are not effective in delivering the news. This is great for consumers because all of this information is free. This is terrible for magazine publishers because subscription rates are down substantially over the last few years. There are better non-profit fundraisers available.

One of the better fundraising ideas for non-profit organizations is raffles. Raffles are great because they are fun and cheap to enter. When you are holding a raffle, you have to make sure you're offering a great prize. The latest tech gadgets are always great. IPad, video game systems, laptops, and other electronic devices work the best. The only disadvantage to holding a raffle is that you need a lot of people to buy tickets to make any significant money. If only a few people buy tickets, you are not going to make any money with this.

When it comes to fundraising ideas for non-profit organizations, the best-performing programs I have seen work for any group are coupon books. There are several versions of coupon book fundraisers you could use with your non-profit organization. Some of the books include coupons to a specific restaurant or group of restaurants. Other coupon books are entertainment coupon books that include coupons for all sorts of entertainment venues.

The best performing coupon books include discount coupons to major retailers. This is because major retailers like Target and Wal-Mart sell products that appeal to every age demographic.

The best fundraising ideas for non-profit organizations should appeal to everyone. When you have a product that sells itself, the youth will be motivated to sell it! When they see how many people buy the coupon books, they will be motivated to sell more books!

Importance of Fundraising For Non-Profit Organizations

Fundraising is a vital part of a non-profit organization. In addition to the people that receive service and those that provide the service, having adequate funds is the fuel that keeps your cause moving. Without money, often resources will prove to be very limited and people that service will be inconsistent. You may even start to see your cause begin to lack focus and interest in the community. Raising and receiving funds allows you to be more innovative which keeps your creative juices flowing while allowing you to have the confidence that you will not run out of gas.

Fundraising must play an important role in your Marketing Communications Plan (MARCOM) in order to successfully strategize and maximize what you receive. Often organizations don't plan out their vision and just plan as they go. Sometimes they may experience success but often they will not experience the total success as they would if their vision was mapped out in their MARCOM properly. The baby steps that you take are just as important as the big event. Here are several things that are important to include in your MARCOM in order to have focus and clarity around fundraising for your organization. You need to:

- Identify who your major donors are and what types of activities interest them

- Calendar all of your events big and small
- Create your budget for each event
- Develop your team for each event and identify the lead person for each
- Designate how the raised funds will be spent for your organization
- Determine what your financial goals are for each event
- Effectively communicate throughout the year with all of your donors

It is important that if your organization is fundraising, which I hope you are, that you remember to ASK. According to Giving USA, in 2009, in the midst of a recession, total giving was still more than $300 billion. Remember these people want to make a difference and to be a part of a positive change. You have to position your cause in front of them and communicate the value that you give as you serve so that donors can continue to give financial support.

So don't run your organization close to empty and on fumes, you will be certain to burnout. Make fundraising an important part of your cause and include it in your Marketing Communications Plan so that it can keep premium fuel in your tank and move you forward as you serve those that need you most.

Fun with Fundraisers For Non-Profit Organizations

There are many non-profit organizations in our communities. Each organization is providing a unique service or goods that are greatly needed in our society. All of these organizations are holding fundraisers to help them pay for the goods or service they provide. All of the money needed to keep these organizations running must come from members of the community who are willing to give.

Let's face it, not everyone in the community is willing or able to give money to fundraisers held by non-profit organizations. Those who are willing to give are unable to donate to all the organizations asking for their money. It becomes a challenge to hold fundraisers that will attract people and raise the amount of money they need. People like to be entertained and will be more likely to support fundraisers that are fun and unusual. It is also important to keep the cost of the fundraisers as low as possible. After all, you are trying to raise money.

Here are some suggestions for fun, low-cost fundraisers that may help your organization attract more supporters.

Spelling Bee

This is a great, low-cost fundraiser for non-profit organizations. You can invite either children or adults to be the spellers. If you invite children you know their families will support them. If you invite adults their families and friends will come to support them or to heckle them. Either way, you are able to raise funds to meet the financial needs of your non-profit organizations. Each of your spellers gathers pledges for the specific amount the supporter will donate for each word spelled correctly.

For a spelling bee, you will need a room, preferably with a stage for the participants, forms for participants to collect pledges, a spelling list, and a prize or a ribbon for the winner. You may have audience members who have not had the opportunity to make a pledge. Since this is a fundraiser for your non-profit organization you will want to give all audience members the opportunity to fill out a pledge form before the spelling bee begins. I addition to the host you may want to have a panel of judges to help determine if a word is spelled correctly and keep track of how many words each person spells correctly.

Since this is a fundraiser for the non-profit organization you may want to allow the spellers to bribe the judges in order to increase their number is "correctly spelled" words. All bribes go to the organization. It is best to have volunteers collect the money from the pledges immediately following the spelling bee. You may also want to ask volunteers to help provide refreshments. People are more likely to come to an event when they know there will be refreshments.

Dog Show

This is a great, almost free, fundraiser for any non-profit organization. Dogs are very lovable animals and dog owners love to show off their pets. You will need a park or large, grassy yard or a large room in a building that allows dogs. All interested dog owners sign up and pay an entry fee. Funds raised by the entry fee go to the non-profit organization. In order inspire more participation you will want to have several categories for the dogs to compete in, including, smartest, cutest, smallest, largest, most talented, etc. A panel of judges will determine the winner.

Since this is a fundraiser for a non-profit organization you may want to allow people to bribe the judges. All bribes go to the organization. All winners receive a ribbon. Providing refreshments for the human participants is optional, however, you will want to provide treats for the four-legged stars.

Fundraisers using dominated pictures

The non-profit committee decides what type of pictures they want to have in the picture perfect contest. These pictures could be pictures of babies, cute pets, ugly pets, exotic pets, best dads, best moms, vacations, landscape, flowers, or anything in your area people take pictures of. Supporters who want their pictures to be part of the contest need to take the picture to the non-profit organizations the day before the event.

For the fundraiser event, the pictures are posted on a board or wall with a table nearby for the voting. Each picture receives a number. Guests at the fundraiser vote for their favorite picture by buying tickets, writing the number of the picture on the ticket and placing it in the appropriate box. You can have several boxes; cutest, funniest, most talented and grand prize. Guests can buy as many votes as they want to make sure their favorite picture wins. Before the evening ends the votes are counted and a ribbon is placed by the winning pictures. It is also a good idea to have a nice gift for the grand prize winner. This will encourage supporters to submit pictures and come to the event to vote for their picture.

Photo Booth Fundraiser

For this fundraiser, you will need a person who has the equipment to take and develop pictures at the event. This can either be a Polaroid camera or a digital camera hooked to a laptop computer and a printer. You may want to decorate a small area and have costumes ready for guest to have their picture taken. You may have a throne with crowns and robes so guest can dress up like the royal family or western outfits with hay or Santa and his elves. When you use your imagination the possibilities are endless.

If you have a person with the computer and printer that has a photoshop program the pictures can be taken against a green wall. They can then be placed in a background chosen by the guest before printing. I would limit the choices, 3 to 5 choices, or the guests may have a hard time choosing which background they want.

With the technology we have available to us today it is easy to take and print pictures. Even our phones have cameras. With all these pictures around us, a picture perfect fundraiser is a great way to show them off.

Most people I know consider themselves good photographers. They would love a chance to help raise funds for their favorite non-profit organization by sharing their talent with others. Families also love to have their picture taken for holidays. Photo booth fundraises that are centered on holidays give families the opportunity to have their picture taken and support your non-profit organization.

Picture fundraisers will take a little extra time when planning an event. They will also help you raise a larger amount of funds needed to help run your organizations. When people have a good time at a fundraising and have a picture to remember it they will want to attend the fundraiser the next time it is held.

CHAPTER SIX:
How to Build a Website That Grows YOUR NPO

Just like my writing association, set up a website with a good understanding of what potential members and donors want can help you grow quickly by attracting member's right from the internet.

What Potential Members Want

Potential members want three main things:

1. They want to know you have a thriving, engaged community. Research shows the number one reason anyone joins an association is that they want the opportunity to network with like-minded individuals. If you can prove this on your website, there's a great chance someone will join online. You can showcase this by doing the following:
   ∘Including pictures of members and events
   - Member testimonials and quotes about the value your organization offers
   - Information about upcoming events

2. The second most important thing potential members want is access to specialized information or educational content. You can attract new members on your website by publishing industry reports, educational webinars, or creating a members' only section with restricted access to valuable resources.

3. The third thing potential members want is instant access and an easy way to join and pay for things online. Why? Online shopping and same day delivery have made people expect instant gratification from the organizations they interact with. I've seen nonprofits fall behind because they require all new members to download a PDF form, print it out, physically fill it out, and then mail it in — a process that can take a whole week. On the other hand, I've also seen organizations who've modernized this process by allowing new members to join online. The result? An instant increase in members and event registrations (here's the story of a ski club that sold out in record time after accepting online payments).

What Potential Donors Want.

Potential donors also want three things. And the NPO Overall, potential donors want:

1. To know your organization's mission. This lets potential donors know why you exist and why they should give to your organization. In fact, this information is the most important thing potential donors want to know before donating.

2. To know where their donations are going. Research shows the number two thing potential donors' need before making a donation is to feel comfortable about where their donation is going. Including explicit information on the breakdown of what happens to a donation can help increase donations.

3. The last thing every online donor wants is similar to what members want — an easy way to donate. Nothing is more frustrating than multiple steps, downloadable forms, or complicated processes. A simple donation button or form with instant online payments is best. If you're looking for tips to make your own donation page, I've written a full guide here.

If you craft your website with the right information and allow online registration and donations, your website will start to grow your organization for you. This is a concept we talk a lot about because we've seen how drastic the results can be if done right. If you'd like to learn more about how to do this, we have a free webinar called, Turn Your Website into a Membership Growth Engine, which covers:

- Three website changes that will start attracting new members right away
- How to get anyone on your board to easily make updates by themselves (even if they don't have any tech experience)
- The top website features our most successful clients use to drive membership growth.

What Pages your Non-Profit Website Needs to Be Complete.

Now that you have an understanding of what people want, the next thing to do is to build out your website.

From studying hundreds of nonprofit websites, here are the most common pages I've seen:

Homepage

Think of this page as a one-page pitch to get someone to join your organization or donate (so include buttons to join or donate). Besides that, many nonprofits include recent news, featured members, upcoming events, and lots of pictures.

About Us

This is where your mission, vision, history, staff, and general information about your nonprofit goes.

Join Us

This page has all the information about what a new member might need to know before joining your organization as well as the online form to join.

Donate

This page has all the information about what a potential donor needs to know before donating to your organization as well as the online form to donate. Here's a complete guide on how to build this page out.

Events

The best way to make this page is to simply host a calendar of upcoming events where people can register. It's also a good idea to list some benefits of joining one of your organization's events.

News/Blog

This is the area for you to post important updates about your organization. If you need help building up your blog traffic, here's my formula and advice for doing it: How I Quadrupled My Nonprofit Blog Traffic in Less Than 1 Year

Resources (if applicable)

If part of the value your organization creates is from publishing resources, this is the   place to host them.

Member-Only Area (if applicable)

This is where you give restricted access to resources intended for members only.

Contact Us

This page includes basic contact information for your organization.

While these are the most common pages for nonprofit websites (and most websites admittedly), whatever pages you decide to publish, having an organized structure will allow website visitors to find information faster, and can even boost your search engine optimization results. Here are some more tips on how to organize your website.

How To Start An NPO Social Media

That's because Google treats social media profiles with high importance when determining what to show in their rankings. If you take the time to set up social media profiles for your organization, you'll be able to see the same result, which can instantly increase awareness of your nonprofit on Google when you're first starting out.

On top of this, the rise of the internet and smartphones has actually decreased people's attention spans, making it harder for nonprofits to stand out and get their your message across. This means that your organization must have multiple presences across different social media channels. People check Facebook 14 times a day, and if your organization doesn't come up in their feed, they're not going to think of you.

There are three social media platforms that I recommend you setup first for your nonprofit: Facebook, Twitter, and LinkedIn. These social media platforms are some of the biggest and also relatively easy to setup and maintain. Once your social profiles are set up and your website is ready to go, it's finally time to start attracting members.

Conclusion

Thank you again for downloading this book!

I hope this book was able to guide you on how to start your NPO The next step is to take action.

Finally, if this book has been helpful, then I'd like to ask you for a favor, would you be kind enough to leave a review for this book?

It'd be greatly appreciated!

Thank you and good luck!